The "Price" and the Value of Money

A Psychological Study

Dueep Jyot Singh

Science of Living Series

Mendon Cottage Books

JD-Biz Publishing

Download Free Books!

http://MendonCottageBooks.com

All Rights Reserved.

No part of this publication may be reproduced in any form or by any means, including scanning, photocopying, or otherwise without prior written permission from JD-Biz Corp Copyright © 2016

All Images Licensed by Fotolia and 123RF.

Disclaimer

The information is this book is provided for informational purposes only. The information is believed to be accurate as presented based on research by the author.

The author or publisher is not responsible for the use or safety of any procedure or treatment mentioned in this book. The author or publisher is not responsible for errors or omissions that may exist.

Our books are available at

1. Amazon.com
2. Barnes and Noble
3. Itunes
4. Kobo
5. Smashwords
6. Google Play Books

Download Free Books!

http://MendonCottageBooks.com

Table of Contents

Introduction 4

The World Owes Me a Living 13

Money and Happiness 19

The Accumulation of Material Possessions 27

Material Riches – A Story of Some Ray – Bans 31

Job Satisfaction 37

Obsession with Money 41

Conclusion 47

Author Bio 50

Publisher 61

Introduction

Oscar Wilde once said – "A cynic is that person who knows the price of everything and the value of nothing." This was said more than 100 years ago, and I was wondering about how man suddenly decided that his idea of happiness was tied up with the thought of money and why he has become so materialistic.

This book is being written because I have noticed that more and more acquaintances and friends of mine instinctively look at an item in somebody else's house, and start pricing it mentally. Sometimes they even blurt out the price, as if they cannot help it. And the tone is either very envious, or rather patronizing.

So this book is going to tell you all about how you as a human being could start learning about the value of money and its place in the scheme of things. You may also teach your children this particular attitude, and this is going to be explained in further volumes. So that your child does not grow up thinking that the level of his contentment, satisfaction, and happiness as he grows up to be an adult is directly linked with the amount of money in his bank balance, or amounts accessible to him. In fact, you could learn the price of money and the value people put on it, right here.

Believe it or not, more and more psychologists have found out that the level of depression among the younger generation, in nations where the wealth level has tripled due to economic security, in the past century, especially in nations which are industrialized and highly developed, has increased proportionally.

I am a great admirer of Louis L'Amour, even though jealous critics consider his stories to be rather of a sameness. Ordinary man, making good , and good always winning against evil. But they do not see the powerful and underlying power of a way of living, which they of course in all their soft, pampered lives could never have dreamed.

These are the pioneers. These are those hard-working men and women who know the value of hard work, and that is why they know how money is earned through no shortcuts and no dole outs, unless one is a seriously bad man.

I like the Sackett stories the most. The narrator is almost always in the first person, and you can see his own personal life's outlook, in some words said casually. For example, here is one of the Sackett Brothers talking about some of the debts left by his father. The 3 brothers get together, work hard for 2 years and pay off every debt. It is a matter of honor. After the last debt has been paid, they have just their saddles and absolutely not a single red cent and they know that they have to go back to work again.

And they could not care less. That is because, since day one, they know the value of money. They know the price of things. They also know all about the value of everything, because they have learnt it the hard way.

Do they sit down, and ask for their government, or their state or their family members to feed them, clothe them, and take care of them, because they have absolutely no intention of working and earning any money. What happened in 150 – 200 years, from the time of the writing of the Sackett saga, even if it is fictional, and the reality of today, when people are definitely not satisfied with life or contented with what they have, have no intention of bettering their lifestyles through hard work, and instead have reached the state of demanding that they be taken care of, throughout their lives?

So this is where I come into the psychological aspect of how the excess of wealth, and prosperity has changed a culture, a person's state of mental good health, especially in his pursuit of happiness and contentment in his life.

This book is going to tell you all about real life experiences, especially those which you can see all around you, because they are global in nature. This book is also going to tell you all about life rules and principles, especially those followed in ancient times when people were content, with what they had and how they knew that it was in their hands to change their circumstances, state , and conditions of living, lifestyles, and grow more prosperous.

Now let me talk about some stories told to me by my elders. Naturally, all over the World, let us say anywhere between 80 – 150 years ago, money matters were in the hands of the older generation and the experienced. They knew how to stretch a penny so far, that it squeaked. So unless you were seriously rich, and could afford to throw money about, the rest of the World knew all about how to make one cent, pence, or dime earn its full value.

That was the time when everybody thought that it was so nice to be rich, because according to them, those aristocrats and royalty, which were rich, were happy, because they could afford everything they wanted.

That is so not true. If you look at the historical aspect of riches, the aristocrats were prevented from earning their money by their own hands, because noblesse oblige considered that to be a not very blue blooded profession. That is why in a number of generations, they were reduced to marrying money in order to survive, gambling in order to restore the family fortunes or by just trying any other supposedly acceptable manner in which they could fill up the family coffers with gold and silver.

The Emperor was not happy with all his millions, but that really happy man, singing in the garden did not have a shirt on his back. But he knew the secret of contentment. And the reason for his contentment is something which has been written in the Holy Book, but human nature being what it is, man will always want to covet his neighbor's goods.

Ahab, the king of Israel, was rich and should have been contented with what he had. But he wanted the small vineyard of an ordinary man named Naboth. This was Naboth's ancestral land and his children's heritage and that is why he refused to allow the king to pay him a sum for that land or exchange it for a better piece of land. So what did the king do? He came back home, just like a pouting child, and sulked. "Sheol and Abaddon are never satisfied, Nor are the eyes of man ever satisfied."

You may want to ask yourself. Are the rich happier? Not if I go by the affluent couple in this photograph. Not a smile between them and the attitude is so blasé – okay, well, you are gifting me a necklace, so what.

This couple knows the price of the necklace. But they do not know its value because for them it is a status symbol and not a symbol of positive emotions.

And then, here is another great psychological sentence, which goes to the depths of human nature.

"Ahab cannot enjoy Israel, if Naboth enjoy his vineyard."

One is not happy, unless he has what he wants right then. So with his tacit approval, great injustice was done to Naboth and his legal heirs, his sons, who were stoned to death after being accused falsely. And so Ahab managed to justify the taking over of that small vineyard, because after all, the owner was dead.

Naturally, retribution was at hand, and Ahab, even if he repented too late was punished according to his crime, with death in war and his wife Jezebel thrown off the walls of Jezreel.

You may take this story as a historical fact or as a recording of the evolution of mankind, but here are 2 aspects taken at their psychological value. One is man is never satisfied with what he has, and he is always going to be looking for what the other person has, and is never going to be supposedly happy until he has it, either through force, stolen, or bought. The 2nd point is that he is never going to be happy if he sees anybody else happy with what he has. So he is not going to count his blessings for what has been given to him, but is going to wonder why somebody else is so happy, when he does not have what the rich man has, material goods, riches, belongings, treasures, and how dare somebody be happy with just ordinary bread and wine?

Incidentally, this reminds me of another traditional story, taken from the Arabian nights. This is also a very great psychological book, telling all about real human nature.

Once upon a time, in the rich city of Baghdad, lived a caliph. And right under his palace walls lived a gardener and his wife. The gardener sang while doing his work. He earned enough money throughout the day, and his wife was happy and content to make a home for her husband and they were living happily ever after. Until one fine day, the caliph who was definitely not happy, heard the gardener singing.

How is that, he asked the grand Vizier, how can it be that that person, who is so poor, is still satisfied with his lot, without the ambition for more and more riches, which should be the cause of his happiness?

The Vizier stroked his graybeard and said – master of the land, that man is contented with what he has. That is because he has never looked beyond his horizons and aspired to things, of which he could never dream.

The Caliph said pettishly, "Do something about it, can you? I really cannot understand how a person can be happy with so little."

"Oh, that is very easy, Protector of the Poor," said the Vizier. "I just have to put him in the "Whirlpool of 99.""

The Vizier immediately did exactly that. That night, he threw a bag full of 99 gold coins into the garden of the gardener. The gardener found it the next morning. And thus, his sorrows began. Who had given him 99 gold coins? How would he keep them safe from the eyes of jealous neighbors? And why on earth was he given 99 gold coins? There should have been one hundred.

And so the gardener began to strive to earn so much money to complete the bag to a sum of 100 gold coins. Gone were the evening feasts. He and his wife were now concentrating on saving their money and their songs had stopped, because they wanted to earn more and more, and save, so that they could have one hundred gold coins.

So they finally got enough money which could be turned into a gold coin. And then the wife said. Why should we be satisfied with just one hundred gold coins? Why not turn them into 200?

Now, actually, the Arabian night's story stops right here to tell you that the pursuit of wealth and the envy of a rich man was enough to destroy a poor human beings contented way of life.

But older texts, going back to ancient times, has a much happier ending. One fine day the husband came home and told his wife that he had not had soup for 2 years, nor had he tasted fruit, nor had he enjoyed healthy fare, which he was wanted to do, in times when he was not obsessed with the making of money. His wife immediately shrieked at him that no way was she going to spend even one red dinar on wasteful things. She was intent on saving that money to fill up her coffers.

The gardener spent a sleepless night. The next morning, he picked up the bag, and went straight to the Caliph.

"Oh Exalted one, he said, I am just a poor gardener living under the shadow of your palace. Two years ago some evil and wicked person threw an enchanted bag of money through my window. This bag consists of a really hungry and evil djinn who is never satisfied with what he has. He wants me to fill the bag and appease his hunger. And thus has been taken away my happiness, my peace of mind, and my state of contentment. I cannot sing, I cannot eat, and I cannot feel content with my lot at all, because I am so busy earning more and more money in order to fill up this bag for the money hungry djinn. I know that he is never going to be satisfied and will always ask for more. So please, take this money because you are more used to wealth. You can fill up the bag very easily from your treasures."

And he threw the money bag at the bottom of the throne, and bowed himself out. That evening, there was singing and dancing and feasting in the garden of the gardener, without any regrets. Because the bag with the evil djinn and all its ensuing responsibilities had been placed in the hands of the Caliph. Even though I believe the wife must have shouted and yelled. But then if she was a sensible woman, she would have understood how prosperity can change the status, mindset, and psychological behavior of human beings.

It seems, the Caliph and the Vizier finally understood the great lesson being told to them by just a humble gardener, and since then, the Caliph spent all his time doing good deeds for the people of Baghdad, and spending his money instead of accumulating it.

Remember that an increase in wealth does not automatically mean that you are going to feel happy. Personal contentment is a state of mind. Incidentally, this particular point was researched globally by the National Academy of Sciences, – the things they like to waste their money on, researching, and globally! – And they found out that personal satisfaction and contentment was a state of mind.

Incidentally, this book is going to tell you all about people who are under the impression that the World owes them a living. It is also going to tell you all about the materialistic attitude, being absorbed by the children, of the younger generation conscious and subconsciously, where money is supposed to be the be-all and end-all of everything.

So let us take the first attitude first. The world owes me a living.

The World Owes Me a Living

How many of us have that superior attitude, because we have been brought up to think that but we are absolutely not willing to do anything concrete manually or mentally to better our situation? How many of us like to spend hours and hours dreaming of how we can get rich quick, and these are the fools who are always the targets of conmen and fly-by-night companies. But a honest day's work? One really is not mentally and emotionally geared to go out and work for it, because man is basically lazy and a procrastinator. So unless it is absolutely necessary, he is definitely not going to stir himself, but is going to find out ways in which somebody else does the work for him.

In our management studies, this aspect of psychological behavior came under the heading of "delegation of authority!" We were authorizing our juniors to do our work for us! How many of us are doing the same for the people around us, getting them to shoulder our responsibilities and our burdens because we could not be bothered to stir ourselves and do a honest day's work.

It is possible that we have been brought up that way. Well, let me admit it. As children, we had servants to pick and carry after us. And our elders had brought us up as spoiled brats, in a social milieu, where we children did not have to stir ourselves at all in physical labor ever. Whenever my father used to tell my grandmother that we had to be brought up to know all about the dignity of labor, she used to say, "My grandchildren are always going to have servants. Those servants are going to do the work for their masters. They will always be able to afford servants."

I still live in a culture, where servants in the home do all the jobs are the rule and not the exception. However, when I was at college, I began thinking for myself. Here was I, a totally useless specimen, incapable of washing my own clothes, cleaning my own house, cooking, or doing anything on my own, and thinking myself quite an upper crust cookie and quite superior to all those friends and classmates, whose mothers and fathers had not been quite so affluent and thus they had been taught from day one to fend for themselves.

Those people were much more useful than I was. In an emergency, those girls could manage a house, raise a family, and be more practical and constructive human beings than I could ever be. So I began learning how to be useful. All right, so I would have servants, when I grew up and I had a house of my own, but I would not be so helpless that I had to depend on other people in order to take care of my own family when necessary.

Naturally, I think that this is the most adult decision I made at the age of 16, and I have never regretted it. So many of our children are under the impression that there is going to be someone to fetch and carry after them, that they grow up into totally useless drones.

This attitude is getting to be more and more prevalent in modern days, since children have begun to be brought up with the impression that they are kings, princesses and princes, and their parents are there to provide them with everything they desire.

But do not worry, this attitude was prevalent even 4,000 years ago and I am going to tell you another story about this particular attitude of human beings. A mendicant sat outside the walls of Baghdad, and because he was a holy man, every passerby handed him a dinar. The mendicant did not bother to look at the money collected in front of him. And at the end of the day, he walked away with all that money lying on the ground.

There was a shop keeper, who saw this unusual proceedings, and said, "Oh, holy one, why didn't you gather up all the offerings that had been offered to you by the passersby?"

The mendicant looked at him with a very patronizing look, and said in a very hearty and superior tone – "because that money was not worthy of me - *Pidram Sultan Bood* – My father was a sultan, so I should have been given offerings of gold and silver!"

We as kids loved this story, which had been told to us by our father. In fact, we went through a phase, when we used to call him Pidram- pater or father – or Sultan, when he was being a bit too arrogant and bossy and laying down the law, a bit too often.

Incidentally, up to the age of 8, we did not know anything about pocket money. There was no question of us being given any sort of pocket money, because the pocket money culture was definitely not something in our particular society at that time.

Children were fed, clothed, and given what they needed, as long as the adults knew that they required those items. These included comics and tasty treats, which were bought, depending on whether the child deserved it or not. But naturally, these were never given to us in excess, because that would spoil us! But the idea of giving money in the hands of children was never prevalent in the East, because money matters were purely adult matters.

And that is the reason why when I was at school I use to see the Convent tuck shop being invaded by a number of my classmates, who bought bubblegum and peanut brittle and shared it with all their friends. And so they had their own coterie of fair weather friends. Unfortunately, that was how their future adult life would be set. They had plenty of access to lots of money, and for them, good friends meant for those who could feed them with tuck and vice versa.

I did not have any pocket money of my own, but luckily I had some of my friends whose parents were sensible enough not to give them any money. We managed with our packed lunch boxes and fruit. And our friendship definitely was something stronger, because it was not based on tuck being shared among our more prosperous acquaintances.

I was in 3rd grade, when I saw a classmate, pouting away. She was sulking, because she had demanded a bite of the ice cream cone – "give me a bite, give me a bite" – of her best friend M., and that selfish, greedy, mean, [this word was very common among that particular group; anybody who did not share anything was "mean"] M had eaten the whole ice cream herself!

Naturally, I was astonished. M. had bought that ice cream for herself. S. did not consider that a factor. She wanted a bite, when she had demanded it and she wanted it right then. M. had refused her, the bad girl, by turning her back on S. S. had a rip-roaring tantrum.

I came back to my best friends, A. N, and the twins, and I asked them why human beings behaved so. Remember, we were in 3rd grade. N. said, "It is a good thing we are not their friends because we would then have to buy ice creams for them and they would eat them all without our getting any bites."

Out of the mouth of babes. I would not be surprised that S. today is still pouting away and demanding from all her acquaintances and her friends that she be given what she wants. Right now. Otherwise she is not going to be their friend. Such people never grow up. Unfortunately, one can only blame S's parents for her attitude towards other people's possessions, and also I was certain that she would have left M. high and dry, when she found that M was not willing to share her ice cream, bubblegum, or peanut brittle with anybody else.

Unfortunately, I am horrified to see that a large percentage of my acquaintances out there are still demanding "bites." Out of things for which they have not paid and they have no intention of doing so. Somebody else has to pay the bills for them.

These are the people who know the price of everything and the value of nothing. For them, money and the easiest source of it, which can provide them with the luxuries to which they are accustomed, without their having to lift a finger, is the basis of their whole existence.

Money and Happiness

Remember, that as they say, money does not buy happiness, but it is necessary to provide you with your basic needs, as well as give you a little bit of security and cushion for other luxuries. But the moment you find yourself getting more prosperous, especially when you are not used to money in the first place, – in the West, this has been called the middle-class society – people start getting to be more money conscious, status conscious, and ridiculously snobbish.

Nevertheless, however much they may become prosperous, they are always going to have the fear that one fine day, they are going to lose their money and all the supposed social status brought to them by their prosperity. What they do not understand is that they are held in contempt by people who have been brought up, as they say in the purple, with a prosperous background going back a number of generations, and all their airs and graces are tolerated, as long as they have money to spend and show off with.

In the 30s and 40s, there was a very popular cartoon newspaper strip known as Bringing up Father. There was this Irish bricklayer, who was an immigrant to America named Jiggs, and suddenly he became very prosperous through winning a million-dollar sweepstake. Suddenly his otherwise sensible wife, Maggie, became a pain in the neck because she wanted to make a splash in American society.

His daughter is tolerable, but his son who could have been something if his father had remained a bricklayer but is now a useless parasite, snobbish, trying his best to fit in with the crowd which is more prosperous, obnoxious, and an insufferable spendthrift. Jiggs wants to go back to his working-class lifestyle, where he can drink plenty of beer and eat plenty of cabbage, while his wife wants him dressed up to the nines to prove that he is a gentleman and thus she is a lady.

This comic strip came into existence in the early 1900s, when one could almost say, working-class immigrants with their own ethics and culture were trying to assimilate in American society, and making a hash of it. They were definitely not "lace curtain," but wanted to be thought so.

And so vaudeville and cartoons had an amusing time lampooning them, their behavior, and their attitudes. And once they got a little bit of money, and became what they thought was upwardly mobile, they tried very hard to fit in with the Joneses, who definitely found them very amusing.

In fact, I remember reading a classic of the 1930s, when a group of these ladies in Baltimore had started their own club, and only those people could become members, whose genealogy went back to European royalty! Interesting, that these immigrants who were working-class peasants, even indentured servants, who had escaped from England and had reached America to start a new, more prosperous life there found that 4 generations later, they would be having children who were spending money to prove that they came from Bourbons, Capets, and Royal European ancestry! And these women addressed each other in the club as "Your Grace, My Lady, Contessa," and so on.

They knew very well that 4 generations ago, their ancestors had either escaped Europe due to religious persecution, or because the law had decided that England/Europe did not need them and they had better go and colonize America the way convicts were transported to Australia and plantations in the Dutch Indies and so on.

But even so, psychologically, they were definitely not proud of their own plebeian origins and wanted to prove to the World around them that they were of superior blood much more than the common herd. This is a natural instinct, and a person is going to do that wherever he goes, pretending to be what he is not.

I remember reading Booth Tarkington's The Conquest of Canaan, where a young man goes away to college, and comes back home in triumph, telling everybody that he had been a great man on the campus.

And his step brother recounts what happened next to his little friend, Ariel –
"Gene made me unpack his trunk and I do not believe he is as great a man at
college as he is here. I opened one of his books and someone had written in
it, *Prigamaloo Bantry the Class "Try to Be."* He had never noticed and you
ought to have heard him go on. You would have just died Ariel, I almost
bust wide open. It was a mean trick in me, but I could not help showing it to
him."

There are so many of us Prigamaloo Bantrys out there, hiding the feeling of
inferiority and inadequacy by boasting, and talking about our backgrounds
or even about our financial wealth.

And these people are of course very touchy about their supposed blue
blooded ancestry. So one day, when I found one of my friends in Boston,
talking about another friend, whose great great great grandmother had
supposedly come over to America in the original Mayflower, and that is
why she belonged to the great families of Boston, and I tactlessly said – me
with my big mouth – whether that woman was an indentured servant, or a
farmer's daughter or a seamstress or what, I was subjected to a goggle eyed
stare.

Because according to the history I had read, the Mayflower just had 200 or
so people sailing on it, and not one of them came from the supposed middle-
class or upper-class society of Europe of that time.

T. is still not talking to me. What did I mean by telling her that her great-
grandmother did not belong to an aristocratic background, but was working-
class?

This feeling of social inferiority still lurks somewhere in the hearts and
minds of many people whose ancestors were immigrants to other lands.

They do not want to say proudly that these people came, worked with their hands, worked with pride, and made their mark on a society which grew strong on their culture, their ethics, their beliefs, and their traditions. However once they grew prosperous, that did not automatically bring about a culture or a background, when they did not have the basic education, training, or tutelage to act in a proper manner. Nor did they have the breeding.

And so they made their presence felt, by either patronizing brashness, loud crude behavior, boasting about their high connections and their exalted blood and breeding, trying to go into high society and making brash remarks like "our daughters are duchesses." By the way, this particular remark was followed with a retort of "your daughters may be duchesses, but their fathers are clerks, and their brothers are shop keepers."

This attitude continued up to the early 1920s and even 1930s, when New York decided to have the upper 400, when these upwardly mobile people try to get their sons and daughters married into a social stratum, which they considered to be higher than theirs. I remember one of my favorite books, by LM Montgomery – <u>The Blue Castle</u>, where the hero's father becomes a multimillionaire through inventing some liniments and pills and the hero becomes engaged to a so-called society beauty.

http://gutenberg.net.au/ebooks02/0200951h.html

He happens to eavesdrop by accident on a discussion between his future wife and her friends, with her true opinion about him.

"I thought she loved me. I was fool enough to think that. I was wildly happy when she promised to marry me. For a few months. Then—I found out she didn't. I was an involuntary eavesdropper on a certain occasion for a moment. That moment was enough. The proverbial fate of the eavesdropper overtook me. A girl friend of hers was asking her how she could stomach Doc. Redfern's son and the patent-medicine background.

"'His money will gild the Pills and sweeten the Bitters,' said Ethel, with a laugh. 'Mother told me to catch him if I could. We're on the rocks. But pah! I smell turpentine whenever he comes near me.'""

Unfortunately so many of us are so covered with gild and so proud of the fact that we are rich that we do not know that our friends are subconsciously smelling the turpentine when they come near us. And that is because we have been showing off a bit too much about how prosperous we are, and hoping against hope that that is going to be enough for them and garner us inclusion in their own particular magic social circle and level of society.

One of the loveliest of American beauties, Consuelo Vanderbilt, was married off to a British Duke, who detested all things American, but definitely did not mind his American wife's dollars. The 19-year-old Consuelo did not want to marry him, but her ambitious mother, – who was herself of a cotton factor's daughter, and thus considered to be common blood – forced her into an unhappy, loveless marriage, because her daughter would be a Duchess and mother dearest imagined herself in the courts of St. James, among British high society, boasting about my daughter, The Duchess.

It was after Consuelo was married off to the Duke of Marlborough – she was Winston Churchill's aunt by marriage and the marriage settlements in the hands of the Duke – her mother was told firmly by his mother. "Madame, your daughter is now the Duchess of Marlborough, but that does not mean that you can presume to visit her whenever you want, or to come to any social affairs, where she is going to be invited. So you can stay in New York and talk about your daughter, The Duchess, but you have no place in London!"

Mrs. Vanderbilt's idea of happiness was that her money would bring her social prominence and her daughter, lots of joy and happiness, but instead, she had handed over her daughter and her dollars – $2.5 million in those times, equivalent to $68 million of today's currency – to a ruthless woman, who knew exactly what she was doing.

Selling her son and his title to the largest bank account available. The marriage lasted from 1895 to 1921 when it was annulled. One is only glad to say that Consuelo's 2nd marriage was a very happy one, and the Duke's 2nd marriage to Consuelo's American best friend was as miserable as it could get, with the 2nd Duchess, insulting him at every opportunity and ridiculing him whenever she could.

Nobody can dream of the chagrin in the soul and heart of Mrs. V, who spent the rest of her life, smiling bravely, and talking about her daughter The Duchess, in whose life she was never allowed to interfere, take part or even contact ever again, once she was married.

So you can understand the psychological aspect of the power of money in our lives. It is the possession of this money, and how it influences the opinion of people all around us, and our standing in society, which we consider to be instrumental in gaining us plenty of happiness. This is of course an ephemeral idea.

That is because we have some sort of mental and emotional satisfaction that we are somewhat higher in the pecking order, in society, much above the rest. And that is why we also think that if you had a bit more money, we would be on another social level, and that is why we need to have that much money. And that is going to supposedly make us happier. What we do not know is that we spend so much time, trying to keep up with the Jones's, and envying somebody else's prosperity, and trying our best to earn lots and lots and lots of money that we have absolutely no chance or time for personal happiness!

The Accumulation of Material Possessions

I was reading one of Jack London's classic stories, where the richest man in the Eskimo tribe had 24 fishhooks. Just imagine the idea of prosperity, where prosperity was bound up with material items which could provide his family with 24 fishes at a time. Naturally, when the trader reached there with his own pile of goods, which nobody else had seen he also brought unhappiness, discontent, and disharmony in a once happy land.

Now you have decided that you need a little bit more money, because you think that it is tied up with your idea of happiness. Even 10% more, according to you is going to make all the difference between money matters, worries, and contentment, according to you.

You are not going to win the sweepstakes. You will have to go out and look for alternative sources of income, which can get you that 10%. Most of us are definitely not willing to make that effort, and spend our lives, saying that if we only had a little bit more money, we would have been happier. What we do not know is that we wasted all that precious lifetime, which could have been used positively, and in a happier manner, by whining, complaining, sulking, and making ourselves feel envious and jealous, instead of doing something constructive in order to alleviate that scarcity of material goods and money.

Now let me come to one very important psychological aspect of filling your house up with all those expensive doodads and fancy goods. For a while, you have plenty of mental satisfaction that you can afford all these things. And then suddenly you want more. Believe it or not, half of the shopaholics that you know, are already on this materialistic treadmill, and they have to shop, and they have to buy, in order to get some sort of physical, mental, and emotional satisfaction.

You may not notice that these people do not have anything constructive to do. Either they are so rich, that they have never needed to go out and earn in their own money or they are compulsive buyers and are badly in debt or they have absolutely no idea of the value of money or even of budgeting.

According to them, they get an emotional boost, whenever they buy something new which they can afford. And then the packet is put in the cupboard and forgotten, because at that time they wanted it, and once they have possessed it, they do not think they need it anymore.

Think about it. You are so absolutely happy with that new jazzy car that you have bought. You feel really proud when you drive it on the streets, and see people admiring it. One year later, it is just a car, and new models are out, and other people are driving them, and you are wondering how to upgrade your car, so that you can look at the glint of envy yet once more in the eyes of your neighbors.

Psychologically, it has been proven that human beings who spend their money for the good of others or in charitable purposes are emotionally healthier and happier than those people who are busy spending their money buying things for themselves. But most of us just hate the idea of giving the money away to charity, when we would rather buy something which makes a splash in society and in a really conspicuous fashion. This is natural and inborn and an innate instinct in human beings. So do not feel ashamed of it. Any normal, healthy person is going to give it to this instinct, sometime or the other in his life!

Material Riches – A Story of Some Ray – Bans

Here is a story about my wanting something, being human, but not making it the be-all and end-all of my contentment. And just because I never bothered much about those things, I got them in plenty, and in the fullness of time.

It was 2002 and I was posted in an area where I could not get a management or an administrative job, so I took up a teaching job as something to keep me busy and occupied. In keeping with the culturally ethos and tradition of this particular land, especially with serving families, a majority of my friends, and colleagues were also Army or Air Force wives, whose husbands were away on their duty nonfamily postings and the wives had taken up teaching jobs in the schools, where their children had been enrolled as students.

At that time, Ray-Ban sun glasses were very much en vogue, very expensive, and a definite status symbol, – especially when they had been garnered from pilot or Army officer husbands – to be worn on one snooty nose, and poked ever so often with one superior finger!

I did not have a pair of Ray bans , at that time. But because I am a healthy hundred percent red-blooded human being with the naturally acquisitive instincts of millions of years and generations of savages behind me, naturally, I also wanted one of these fashionable accessories.

Apart from that, I also wanted to come out of the school at the end of classes, take out my Ray-Bans, perch it on my haughty nose, as I took out my keys from my Gucci purse and drove away in a cloud of Chanel number 5. Brand names and expensive fashion accessories were the name of the game, at that time too, as they are today. The Gucci was there, the Chanel number 5 was there, but where were the Ray Bans?

I remember thinking very clearly – "So, one day I am going to have a pair of Ray Bans of my own. This was just a random thought and a subconscious aspiration, but it was definitely not tied up with my notion of happiness! And I had definitely not made it a mental or emotional issue, but had this satisfaction that one day I would possibly decide to buy one on my own, or if not, so what? I would not die of deprivation if I did not have a pair.

Two years later, my brother decided to present me with a really really expensive pair for an un-birthday present, just because he felt like presenting his sister with something and just because he has a generous nature.

So the next time he came on his annual leave with his family and spend a month with his sister and all the other relatives gathered together, he had a pair of really, really expensive Ray Bans in his pocket for sister, followed up with a really hearty hug.

All of us were on vacation and all of us had gathered together as we did annually from all corners of the compass. My aunt with her family from California, was also spending her annual holiday at our home at the same time.

And she said, "Aha, that reminds me." She had a pair of one-of-a-kind Ray Bans, of which only 200 had been made. She had bought those Ray Bans for me – or perhaps for herself, or had perhaps been gifted that pair, I still do not know!– and I immediately commandeered them, chirping, "Thank you, thank you, thank you" and she could not say hey, no!

I immediately took off the glasses presented to me by my brother and put on those gold rimmed classy looking status symbols. I might have preened a bit too. And then I looked at his face, which had gone strangely quiet.

He had bought those Ray Bans for me with such love, and here I was cooing over something which was about 4 times more expensive , and was possibly the only one of its kind, in the city/possibly country, at that time. Aunt had somehow, with her unfortunate timing managed to rain upon his particular parade.

I immediately told aunt that I thanked her for her gift, which I really, really loved, but which I would be using on very very select and rare occasions when I wanted to act really snobbish and superior among equally obnoxious snob and superior snooty beings!

But for everyday use, my brother's Ray Bans were what I was going to use forever and ever. And they are still going strong today. So are the gold rims.

My brother grinned, pointed to the gold rims, and told me that I could give those to him in exchange! What would I do with 2 pairs? According to aunt, that chap Tom Cruise had a pair- so what? They would look equally stylish on brother's hawk nose too, especially when he was glaring over their edges, yelling at his subordinates and juniors.

As a response, he got beat up with pillows and cushions by his loving sister and his cousins, – ably assisted and supported by the enthusiastic mutt- while his wife, baby son, grandmother, aunt, and other relatives looked on and giggled away.

I still remember those magic moments which are really precious, because that was the last family gathering, when all of us would be together but we did not know it at that time. Five precious members were lost to us unexpectedly and in an untimely fashion within the next 2 years.

More than 15 years have passed since I was given these gifts. They may have their own very expensive material value, but for me, the memories associated with them are much more precious. Also, they are cherished emotionally, because they were presented to me by loved ones.

So remember that material goods that you buy for yourself may give you some emotional or mental satisfaction, but if they have really happy memories associated with them, they are going to be even more precious.

However, if you spend your hard earned money on experiences which give you happier memories, you are going to feel more happy and satisfied. You have the moments of laughter, to reminisce over, especially when you look at the photographs of those precious days, 20 years later.

However, if you spend all that money, buying material goods, which are just going to be packed away, one fine day, you are going to ask yourself, oh my, I spent $2,000 on that bit of rubbish?

Remember that experiences, which allow you plenty of happy social interaction, creating happy memories, and strengthening your relationships, social ties and other activities are more valuable in your spiritual and emotional growth than those materialistic things which like hungry djinns in the bag need to be upgraded and fed every day!

My mother recounts some more incidents of our childhood, of which of course I do not remember anything. According to her, when all the friends of the neighborhood used to come to my house to play, and it was time for them to go home, I use to hand over all my toys to them because they did not have them, and I had them. I was about 6 and a half years at that time. Remember, children do not have a natural instinct of acquisitiveness in them until it is taught to them.

On the other hand, there was my little 4-year-old brother standing right at the gate and confiscating all the toys, which had been given away in largess by his heedless, reckless sister.

One day my grandfather saw him doing that and asked him why he was taking those toys back. This is what this practical little boy said, "if all the toys are given away, they are not going to come back again to play with us."

Grandpa was astounded! In fact, he went around telling all of his friends about what his little grandson had learned for himself at the age of 4, what it took grandpa 62 years to learn!

Now this is a part of instinctive human nature, which that little child knew deep inside. Where did a 4-year-old boy learn that? At that time he recognized the fact that human beings were quite capable of looking for new pastures, especially more prosperous ones, when the source of one particular prosperous pasture dried up.

So many decades have passed since then. But subconsciously, he knows that human beings are innately greedy, selfish, materialistic, and he could not care less about the fact that most of his acquaintances are fair weather friends. He has a couple of dear friends, which stick closer than a brother, through thick and thin and according to him, those friendships are worth all the dead wood sticking on like peaches and leeches wherever he goes.

But then, he is much more tolerant than I in matters of human psychology and nature. And that is why he is much more settled, and contended, than a number of his friends. Because he knows about the frailty of human nature and its psychology.

Job Satisfaction

One day, I was collared by a relative, who was really amazed at why I had spent my professional life taking up a number of jobs in different fields. If I had stuck to my first job today, I would be the CEO or perhaps the managing director of the company. I could also command my own pay packet anywhere on earth, with that sort of experience, know-how, and knowledge.

In answer I told her that that exalted position and prospect definitely did not please me, even if it made me a multimillionaire, I would be miserable, stressed out, full of tension, and perhaps so ambitious that I would have absolutely no time for my family and other parental and filial responsibilities.

Think it over. Are you happy with your job? Seriously speaking, most of us are going to say, no, not exactly, but as it brings in the monthly paycheck and we have family responsibilities, we are going through the boring 9-to-5 routine every day.

It is this responsibility which has tied us to our desks. In 25 years of working hard and earning my own money, I had 14 jobs in different career fields and all of them were steps- ups. Not many human beings can say that. But then I was fortunate. I had the knowledge. I had the experience. I had the ability to step in any job, learn about it in 10 months, or about 1 ½ years and then decide that it was time for me to move on and try out something new, in some other field.

Many of us do not have this sort of option today. In fact, we cannot dare to take the chance that we may be unemployed, because then who is going to pay the bills, and take care of the expenses of raising a family and managing a house?

Here are the 4 points which gave me plenty of job satisfaction. Every job that I had utilized all my strengths. And best of all, I liked what I was doing at that time. I never woke up in the mornings, saying, oh God, I have to get to the office, what a boring day ahead. The moment I began to think that, I knew it was time for me to move on, and look for another challenge. Also, the jobs which I had always provided me with a sense of being in charge of things and in control.

For the last 15 years, I was often top boss, answerable only to myself. The job was never such that it caused me plenty of tension or stress. I knew the goal I had in front of me, and it was never such that it stretched out my capacities – professional, emotional, mental, spiritual, or physical.

And that is why I consider myself to be lucky, because I was flexible enough to use my capacities for the best professional and financial results.

So remember, if you cannot get out of your dead-end job, try to make it more interesting. Do not be an automaton. Some people with no imagination enjoy a lifetime of monotonous systematic routine work, because according to them, that is the only way things have to be done, should be done, or they have been trained to do them.

Such people retire at the age of 56 or whenever, depending on your location on the globe, with a pension and spend the rest of the time wondering how to occupy their suddenly empty lives. They have never taken up hobbies or some sort of activities which would keep them healthy, happy, and well occupied. These are the people who are going to start suffering from Alzheimer's really fast, because of a steady mental deterioration.

On the other hand, those people who know how to shuttle work, along with constructive relaxation doing something with their hands, are going to feel much more satisfied emotionally, mentally, and physically at the end of the day.

How many of us come straight home from office, throw our shoes at opposite walls, [– unless we are suffering from OCD when we are going to remove our shoes carefully, align them properly, take off our socks, turn them inside out, fold them up, tuck them in our shoes and place the shoes in their allocated place in the shoe rack – how utterly boring –] and then switch on the TV to spend hours and hours watching pictures flicker on the screen, without even bothering about exercising our brain or our body muscles into doing some other more constructive activity.

In our way, we are happy. The day's work has been done. We are relaxing in our own way, unless we are confirmed workaholics. Which means that we are incapable of relaxing, and we are going to spend even this little time out for relaxing thinking up ways and means in which we can wheel a deal, put one over the competition, or earn a little bit of money. This is where I come to another great psychological aspect.

Money money money – I want more.

Obsession with Money

Believe it or not, I have known a lot of people out there, who are so obsessed with money that they spend their whole lives filling up their bank balances. For them, money means security. They may have some explanation that they have had a very hard childhood, and have felt the lack of money acutely, sometime or the other in their lives.

Well, believe it or not, 99.8% of us out there have been through this phase in some form or the other, if we had anything to do with money and the earning of it. If we had an unlimited source of income coming in, and not having to lift a finger to earn it, that is another case, but then you would not be reading this book. This book is for you, I, and for all those people who have often felt, that they could do with a little bit more money.

And most of us set about trying the best way in which we could alleviate that cash flow problem, to the best of our ability. At the age of 80, we are not going to look back on a life which we spent whining and saying, if he had a little bit more of money. Instead, we may feel happy that we managed to earn that much money to fulfill our dreams, give our children the education we had dreamt for them, see them well-settled, and useful human beings, and all through our own efforts.

Notice that in the first instance, we are so self-centered, that we keep talking about how a little bit more of money would have changed our lives. On the other hand, that of a more fulfilled life, we have been doing something constructive for the good of others.

At the same time, we are definitely not going to be so obsessed with money that it was and is the be-all and end-all of our reason for living. I know many people in their 70s and 80s, who have been brought up in hard times. And that is why for them, money is still the only thing which can make them feel secure.

That reminds me of one of these elders who was famous in the city as a living example for this traditional aphorism – *you can flay my skin away, but you are not getting a dime out of me today* – and his excuse whenever anybody asked him why he was not willing to spend any money on himself or on his family was because he was worried about their futures, and his own old age. If they spent money when they were young, they had less of money for when they were old.

He had 2 sons and a daughter. And they were the talk of the town, because even though they belonged to a comparatively affluent family, they had done nothing in their lives, which according to him, cost money, which included going out on social occasions – one needed to buy a new dress, a present and worst of all, one had to repay that social occasion with an expensive party of one's own – and such things, which he associated with money and the spending of it.

Most of us are careful about money, sometime or the other in our lives. But on the other hand, when one reaches the stage that he begins to price everything around him and to tell everybody how he could have bought it 25% cheaper, at some other place and they were not brought up right, and did not know the true value of money, he begins to get a bit tiresome.

So one day, his eldest son had enough. He spent his whole pay packet in clothes for his siblings, and plenty of tasty food for the kitchen, and plenty of pretty useless little amusing nickshicks, just for the heck of it, and things which his mother had wanted for years. When he came home, the head of the family had a fit.

"Give me one good reason why I should not have a standard of living commensurate to my position in society, father?" said the son when the father started screaming about his son's extravagance.

Because, said the father repeating his perpetual instinctive state of mind – "if you spend a lot of money today, what are you going to have when you grow old? And he began whining about his childhood when he had seen really hard times."

The son just squared his shoulders and said, "Father, you had a hard time because you had 13 siblings and your father was a schoolmaster. I have just 3 siblings and my father is an engineer, with a high status high paying job. But living by your own personal standard, and the standard which you expect from your family, we would be better off, living in your little city, on a very limited income, and just dreaming about things we could not have, like you did when you were a child. And you intend all of us to remain in that same state for the rest of our lives. Sorry, no can do."

His father stared at him. "But, but, but," he began to stutter, "if they became extravagant spendthrifts, what would become of them in the future? He was collecting all this money for his children."

His 2nd son, who is a teacher said quietly – *if thy son is a bad one, so why gather all this money for him? If thy son is a good one, why gather all this money for him?*

Since then, he began to change his ways a bit, and stopped thinking so much of money money money. About 4 months later, I met the wife of the 3rd son at a social gathering, – all of them decided to throw off the tyranny of the money obsessed elder and live their own lives – and she had something very amusing to recount to all of us.

The 8-year-old grandchild had gone exploring the dustbins of the neighborhood! And there he had found a pair of really dilapidated and horrible looking slippers. He immediately brought them home, and told his father to repair them, so that grandpa could wear them. Someone had thrown them out, but they had cost money.

Grandpa never liked the idea of money being wasted ever.

Grandpa was horrified, grandpa was shocked. He wear slippers taken from somebody else's dustbin? But, said the little boy reasonably, "Grandpa, you are the one who keeps saying that we have to make do with what we have. I found these old slippers for you. Use them. They will fit you and you have not spent any money on them." And he grabbed his grandfather's well-worn hushpuppies, and made off with them.

And then he went straight to his mother and yelled, "Do you know, mom, the neighbors who have come in that house over there have dustbins full of things which they throw out. You will not need to buy anything from now on. Grandpa will not need to grumble about the prices."

Grandpa spent a really quiet evening, thinking about people's opinion about him. He thought he was being so responsible and mature and thinking of the good of his family. And all the time, he was depriving his own family of the basic requirements needed by them, food, and clothing and other essentials. And the 8-year-old grandchild was thinking of augmenting these items by rootling in the neighborhood dustbins.

I think he woke up that day. He has begun to mend his ways a bit. That 8-year-old kid is a very active, enthusiastic, and boisterous 10 year old today. And whenever grandpa begins "My, this is so expensive, I do not think we need it," he retorts, "do not worry grandpa, I might just find this in somebody's dustbin, do not worry, you do not have to spend a single cent on it," in a loud and clear voice, especially in public, he goes all red and squirms in embarrassment, especially when the people around him smile audibly.

So, possibly, you may be the subject of such audible smiles, especially if you are so money minded that you are depriving your family of things they need so that they have enough of money in the future. You are not being responsible. You are just being miserable. However, that does not mean that you go the other way and you spend money liberally on unessential things to show off how generous you are. This is the best way in which you can spoil your children and make them think that you are always going to be their permanent source of continuous income.

Conclusion

This book has given you plenty of knowledge about the psychological power of money supposedly affecting your state of happiness and your social status. Remember that human beings are conditioned to a way of thinking since childhood. However, they should not allow that childhood conditioning to influence the rest of their lives, especially when it comes to a matter of their own and their family's well-being, mental, physical, and spiritual good health.

So read this book and then think carefully about how much money matters to you. Is it influencing your life? Are you obsessed with gathering it? Do you want so many material goods around you that your idea of happiness is all tied up with the possession of all those heavily priced status symbols? How many people around you are busy gathering money so that they can spend it when they are old? They are definitely not going to do that because when they are old, they are going to be even more obsessed with saving up more and more money.

Everybody knows about a female New York millionaire in the 20s and 30s who had inherited a lot of money from her father and her grandfather. She did not know how to spend that money, because if she had lived in the East, one would say, that money was not in her fate. She lived worse than a pauper in one dress, and ate bread and soup, which she got from the Salvation Army free kitchens for people suffering from the Great Depression.

Everybody around her thought that she was also one of their kind who had lost everything in the crash. Her son, of course, went the other way, and the moment she died and he inherited all those millions, spent all that money in riotous living and died bankrupt.

This reminds me of a traditional story about whether you are fated to be rich or not? A God and his consort were hovering over the earth, when the goddess saw a really poor man walking down the dusty path.

She told her husband that he was the provider of good and prosperity to all the people on the earth, so why did not he provide this particular man with lots and lots of material riches?

"Oh goddess," said the God, "it is not in his fate to be rich and spend all that money."

To prove it, he took a bag full of diamonds and threw it in the path of the poor man. There was nobody around so nobody else would pick up that bag. About 10 feet away from the bag, the poor man suddenly said to himself, "I wonder how difficult it is for a blind man to walk, especially on this road," and he closed his eyes firmly, and stumbled his way past the bag full of diamonds, saying to himself, "it is not very difficult at all. "

I am hundred percent sure the God must have told his consort, see, I told you so, in a really triumphant voice, a few seconds later.

So let me tell you, if it is not written in your fate to enjoy your money especially when you have spent so much of time, earning it, it will go to those people who are fated to get it, either your children or the bankers.

You, on the other hand are going to die happy that you have filled your bank accounts with millions of dollars, even though you never got to spend a dollar on yourself or wished to spend a dollar on anybody else. And so you never had a really joyous moment in your life ever, one which had nothing to do with money.

What a happy life, you must have lead! According to you, you know the value of money, but what a price you paid for it. Ah well.

Live Long and Prosper!

Author Bio

Dueep Jyot Singh is a Management and IT Professional who managed to gather Postgraduate qualifications in Management and English and Degrees in Science, French and Education while pursuing different enjoyable career options like being an hospital administrator, IT,SEO and HRD Database Manager/ trainer, movie , radio and TV scriptwriter, theatre artiste and public speaker, lecturer in French, Marketing and Advertising, ex-Editor of Hearts On Fire (now known as Solstice) Books Missouri USA, advice columnist and cartoonist, publisher and Aviation School trainer, ex-moderator on Medico.in, banker, student councilor ,travelogue writer … among other things!

One fine morning, she decided that she had enough of killing herself by Degrees and went back to her first love -- writing. It's more enjoyable! She already has 48 published academic and 14 fiction- in- different- genre books under her belt.

When she is not designing websites or making Graphic design illustrations for clients , she is browsing through old bookshops hunting for treasures, of which she has an enviable collection – including R.L. Stevenson, O.Henry, Dornford Yates, Maurice Walsh, De Maupassant, Victor Hugo, Sapper, C.N. Williamson, "Bartimeus" and the crown of her collection- Dickens "The Old Curiosity Shop," and "Martin Chuzzlewit" and so on… Just call her "Renaissance Woman" - collecting herbal remedies, acting like Universal Helping Hand/Agony Aunt, or escaping to her dear mountains for a bit of exploring, collecting herbs and plants, and trekking.

Check out some of the other JD-Biz Publishing books

Gardening Series on Amazon

Download Free Books!

http://MendonCottageBooks.com

Country Life Books

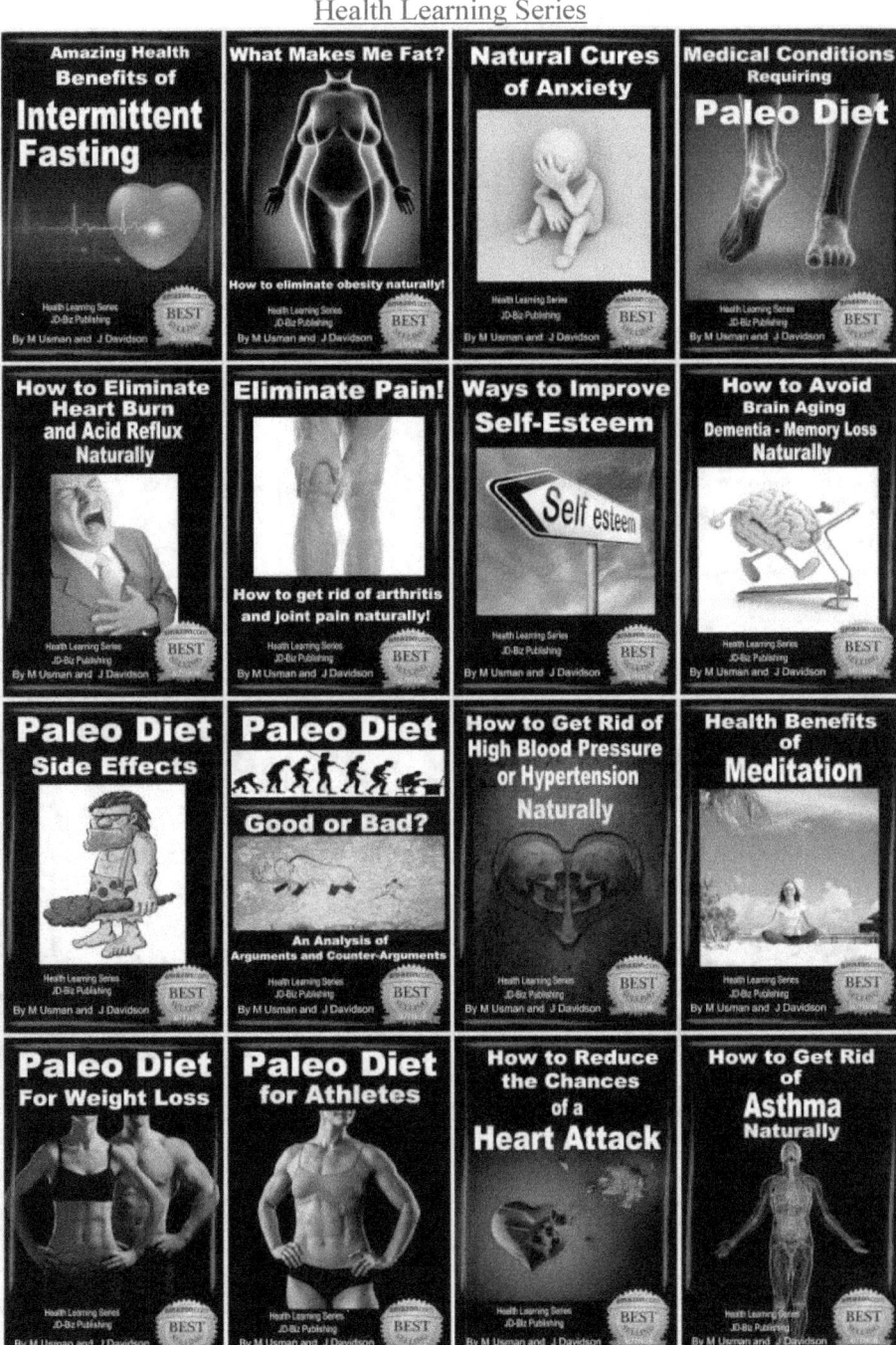

Amazing Animal Book Series

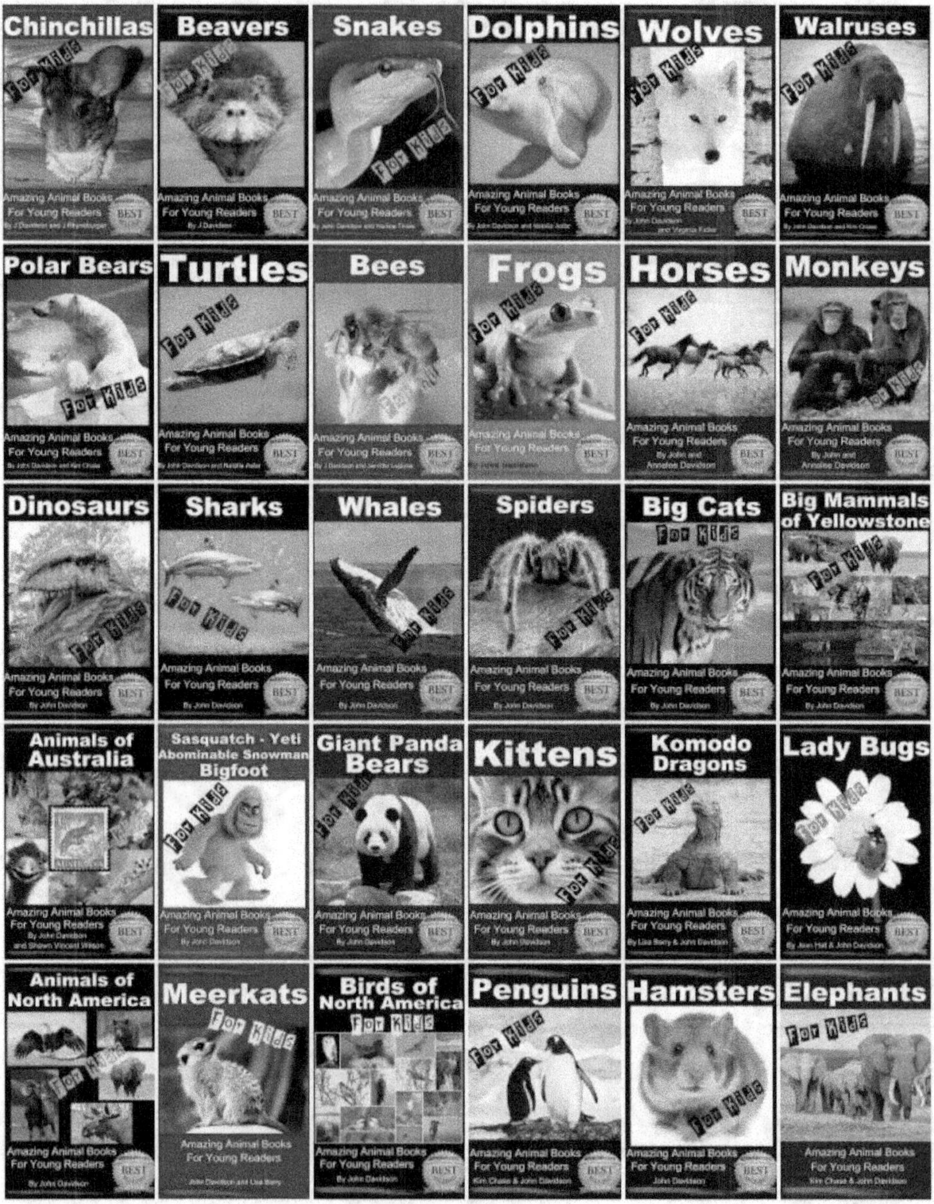

Learn To Draw Series

How to Build and Plan Books

Entrepreneur Book Series

Our books are available at

1. Amazon.com

2. Barnes and Noble

3. Itunes

4. Kobo

5. Smashwords

6. Google Play Books

Download Free Books!

http://MendonCottageBooks.com

Publisher

JD-Biz Corp

P O Box 374

Mendon, Utah 84325

http://www.jd-biz.com/

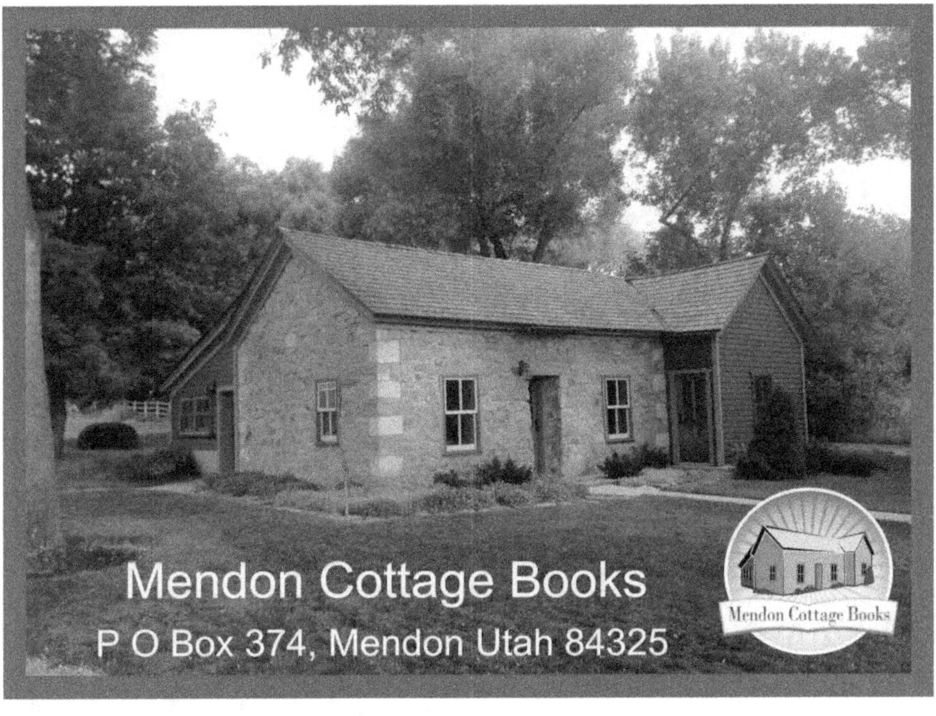

Mendon Cottage Books

P O Box 374, Mendon Utah 84325

www.ingramcontent.com/pod-product-compliance
Lightning Source LLC
Chambersburg PA
CBHW071122280526
45787CB00003B/1141